NOTES ON ENEMY ARMY IDENTIFICATIONS

ITALY

The Naval & Military Press Ltd

October, 1941

Published by

The Naval & Military Press Ltd
Unit 5 Riverside, Brambleside
Bellbrook Industrial Estate
Uckfield, East Sussex
TN22 1QQ England

Tel: +44 (0)1825 749494

www.naval-military-press.com
www.nmarchive.com

*In reprinting in facsimile from the original, any imperfections are inevitably reproduced
and the quality may fall short of modern type and cartographic standards.*

NOTES ON ENEMY ARMY IDENTIFICATIONS

ITALY

PART I

ORDER OF BATTLE

PART II

IDENTIFICATION OF ARMY PERSONNEL

PART III

IDENTIFICATION OF BLACKSHIRT MILITIA PERSONNEL

APPENDICES

CONTENTS

PART I

ORDER OF BATTLE

	Pages
A.—Allocation of Infantry Regiments to Divisions	6–7
B.—Allocation of Artillery Regiments to Divisions	7
C.—Allocation of Alpini Companies and Battalions to Regiments	8
D.—Allocation of Bersaglieri Battalions to Regiments	9

PART II

IDENTIFICATION OF ARMY PERSONNEL

General Notes	10
A.—Uniform (General)	10–11
B.—Badges of Arm and regimental numbers (wearing of)	11
C.—Badges of rank (wearing of)	12
D.—" Pay book " (description)	12
E.—Identity Plate (description)	12
Uniform as worn by officers and other ranks subsequent to June, 1940 (illustration)	13
Italian officers (photographs)	16
Italian infantry soldiers (photographs)	17
Italian troops in shirtsleeves (photograph)	18
Alpini and Bersaglieri head-dresses (photographs)	19
Alpini soldier (photograph)	20
Italian officer in tropical uniform (photograph)	21
Various styles in tropical wear (photographs)	22
Gorget patches and devices (general description)	23
Gorget patches of Infantry Line Regiments	24–29
Gorget devices of Cavalry Regiments	32–33
Gorget patches and devices of Arms and Services other than Infantry of the Line and Cavalry	36–39
Examples of combined gorget patches and devices	41

PART II—*continued*

IDENTIFICATION OF ARMY PERSONNEL—*continued*

	Pages
Badges of Arm of Service	44–52
Badges of rank—Officers	54–56
Badges of rank—Warrant officers and N.C.Os.	58–59
Miscellaneous badges	61–63

PART III

IDENTIFICATION OF BLACKSHIRT MILITIA PERSONNEL

Uniform	64
Branch of Service	64
Badges of rank	65

APPENDICES

A.—Style of uniform prescribed prior to June, 1940	66
B.—Badges of arm, formation and unit prior to June, 1940	68–69
C.—Badges of rank prior to June, 1940	71
D.—Pay books (illustrations)	72–80
E.—Identity plate (illustration)	81
F.—Italian Orders and Decorations	83–85

PART I

ORDER OF BATTLE

A. ALLOCATION OF INFANTRY REGIMENTS TO DIVISIONS.

Regiments.		Division.	
Number	Name.	Number.	Name.
1-2 ...	Re.	13 ...	Re.
3-4 ...	Piemonte.	29 ...	Piemonte.
5-6 ...	Aosta.	28 ...	Aosta.
7-8 ...	Cuneo.	6 ...	Cuneo.
9-10...	Regina.	50 ...	Regina.
11-12...	Casale.	56 ...	Casale.
13-14...	Pinerolo.	24 ...	Pinerolo.
15-16...	Savona.	55 ...	Savona.
17-18...	Acqui.	33 ...	Acqui.
19-20...	Brescia.	27 ...	Brescia.
21-22...	Cremona.	44 ...	Cremona.
23-24...	Como.	14 ...	Isonzo.
25-26...	Bergamo.	15 ...	Bergamo.
27-28...	Pavia.	17 ...	Pavia.
29-30...	Pisa.	26 ...	Assietta.
31-32...	Siena.	51 ...	Siena.
33-34...	Livorno.	4 ...	Livorno.
35-36...	Pistoia.	16 ...	Pistoia.
37-38...	Ravenna.	3 ...	Ravenna.
39-40...	Bologna.	25 ...	Bologna.
41-42...	Modena.	37 ...	Modena.
43-44...	Forli.	36 ...	Forli.
45-46...	Reggio.	30 ...	Sabauda.
47-48...	Ferrara.	23 ...	Ferrara.
49-50...	Parma.	49 ...	Parma.
51-52...	Alpi.	22 ...	Cacciatori delle Alpi.
53-54...	Umbria.	2 ...	Sforzesca.
55-56...	Marche.	32 ...	Marche.
57-58...	Abruzzi.	10 ...	Piave.
59-60...	Calabria.	31 ...	Calabria.
61-62...	Sicilia.	102 ...	Trento (Motorized).
63-64...	Cagliari.	59 ...	Cagliari.
65-66...	Valtellina.	101 ...	Trieste (Motorized).
67-68...	Palermo.	58 ...	Legnano.
69-70...	Ancona.	61 ...	Sirte.
71-72...	Puglie.	38 ...	Puglie.
73-74...	Lombardia.	57 ...	Lombardia.
75-76...	Napoli.	54 ...	Napoli.
77-78...	Toscana.	7 ...	Lupi di Toscana.
79-80...	Roma.	9 ...	Roma.
81-82...	Torino.	52 ...	Torino.
83-84...	Venezia.	19 ...	Venezia.
85-86...	Verona.	60 ...	Sabrata.
87-88...	Friuli.	20 ...	Friuli.
89-90...	Salerno.	5 ...	Cosseria.
91-92...	Basilicata.	1 ...	Superga.
93-94...	Messina.	18 ...	Messina.
95-96...	Udine.	46 ...	Udine.
? 97-98...	Genova.		Genova.
115-116	Treviso.	62 ...	Marmarica.
125-126	Spezia.	45 ...	Spezia.
127-128	Firenze.	41 ...	Firenze.
139-140	Bari.	47 ...	Bari.

Regiments.		Division.	
Number.	Name.	Number.	Name.
141–142	Catanzaro.	64	Catanzaro.
151–152	Sassari.	12	Sassari.
157–158	Liguria.	63	Cirene.
207–208		48	Taro.
? 213–214	Arno.		Arno.
? 217–218		25 bis	Volturno.
225–226	Arezzo.	53	Arezzo.
231–232	Avellino.	11	Brennero.
1–2	Granatieri di Sardegna.	21	Granatieri di Sardegna.
3	Granatieri di Sardegna.	No permanent allocation.	

NOTE.—Companies, both in the infantry and Grenadiers, are numbered consecutively throughout the three battalions of the regiment.

B.—ALLOCATION OF ARTILLERY REGIMENTS TO DIVISIONS

Regiment.	Division.	Regiment.	Division.
1 (Cacciatori delle Alpi).	22	32	32
2 (Metauro)	18	33	33
3 (Fossalta)	16	34	12
4 (Carnaro)	15	35	20
5 (Superga)	1	36	16
6 (Isonzo)	14	37	5
7 (Curtatone e Montanara)	44	40 (Caprera)	31
8 (Pasubio)	9	41	41
9 (Brennero)	11	42 (Sabrata)	60
11 (Monferrato)	3	43 (Sirte)	61
12 (Sila)	55	44 (Marmarica)	62
13 (Granatieri di Sardegna).	21	45 (Cirene)	63
14 (Delle Murge)	23	46 (Trento)	102 (Motorized)
15 (Montenero)	38	47	47
16 (Sabauda)	30	48	48
17 (Sforzesca)	2	49	49
18 (Gran Sasso)	24	50 (Regina)	50
19 (Gavinana)	19	51	51
20 (Piave)	10	52 (Torinc)	52
21	101 (Motorized)	53	53
22 (Vespri)	28	54	54
23 (Timavo)	13	55	27
24 (Peloritana)	29	56	56
25 (Assietta)	26	57	57
26 (Rubicone)	17	58	58
27 (Legnano)	6	59	59
28 (Monviso)	4	131	131 (Armoured)
29 (Cosseria)	37	132	132 (Armoured)
30 (Leonessa)	7	133	133 (Armoured)
		201	
		205	25

C.—ALLOCATION OF ALPINI COMPANIES AND BATTALIONS TO REGIMENTS

Notes.

1. It must be remembered that the Alpini organization is extremely elastic. Battalions (or even companies) may be detached from their parent units and form, with other elements, groups of varying size and composition. Companies and battalions will, however, doubtless maintain their *organic* relations with each other and with their regiments.

2. Second-line battalions have names beginning with "*Val*". Third-line battalions, when formed, have names beginning with "*Monte*".

3. The 10th Alpini Regiment is an association of ex-officers and men.

Regt.	Battalions	Companies	Regt.	Battalions	Companies
1	Ceva	1, 4, 5		Valtellina	246, 248, 249
	Pieve di Teco	2, ?, ?		Val Camonica	250, 251, 252
	Mondovi	9, 10, 11		Val Chiese	253, 254, 255
	Val Tanaro	201, 204, 205	6	Vestone	53, 54, 55
	Val Arroscia	202, 203, 208		Verona	56, 57, 58
	Val d'Ellero	209, 210, 211		Val d'Adige	256, 257, 258
2	Borgo San Dalmazzo	13, 14, 15		Val Leogra	259, 260, 261
	Dronero	17, 18, 19		Val Venosta	? ? 282
	Saluzzo	21, 22, 23	7	Feltre	64, 65, 66
				Pieve di Cadore	67, 68, 75
	Valle Stura	213, 214, 215		Belluno	77, 78, 79
	Val Maira	217, 218, 219		Val Cordevole	206, 266, 276
				Val Cismon (Ski Bn.)	264, 265, 277
3	Pinerolo	25, 26, 27		Val Cima	?
	Fenestrelle	28, 29, 30		Val Piave	267, 268, 275
	Esille	31, 32, 33	8	Tolmezzo	6, 12, 72
	Susa	34, 35, 36		Cividale	16, 20, 76
	Val Chisone	228, 229, 230		Gemona	69, 70, 71
	Val Pellice	224, 225, 226		Val Natisone	216, 220, 279
	Val Cenischia	234, 235, 236		Val Tagliamento	212, 272, 278
	Val Dora	3, 231, 232		Val Fella	8, 269, 270
4	Ivrea	38, 39, 40	9	Vicenza	59, 60, 61
	Aosta	41, 42, 43		L'Aquila	93, 98, 143
	Intra	7, 24, 37		Val Learce	?
	Val d'Orco	238, 239, 240		Val Pescara	285, 286, 287
	Val Baltea	241, 242, 280		Val Tampica	?
	Val Toce	207, 243, 281	11	Bolzano	?
	Monte Rosa	112, 134, 135		Bassano	62, 63, 74
	Monte Cervino (Ski Bn.)	87, 103, 133		Trento	95, 144, 145
5	Morbegno	44, 45, 47		Val Fassa	?
	Tirano	46, 48, 49		Val Brenta	262, 263, 274
	Edolo	50, 51, 52			

D. ALLOCATION OF BERSAGLIERI BATTALIONS TO REGIMENTS

Regiment	Battalions
1	1, 7, 9, 81
2	2, 4, 17, 82
3	18, 20, 25
4	26, 29, 31
5	14, 22, 24
6	6, 13, 19
7	8, 10, 11
8	3, 5, 12
9	28, 30, 32
10	16, 34, 35
11	15, 27, 33
12	21, 23, 36

Note.—The companies are numbered consecutively throughout the regiment.

PART II
IDENTIFICATION OF ARMY PERSONNEL
GENERAL NOTES

1. All particulars given in the succeeding pages refer to *active service* conditions, unless the contrary is expressly stated. Uniforms, badges etc., worn only in peace time or for ceremonial occasions are of little interest to-day.

2. A *five-pointed star* is the distinctive emblem of ALL personnel belonging to the regular armed forces. In the case of the *Army* it is worn on. *each side of the collar.* Whilst usually in white metal, it is sometimes merely embroidered.

3. For the sake of convenience, Italian soldiers of the rank of " maresciallo " are described as W.Os.; those of other non-commissioned rank as N.C.Os. The enemy's own classification is given on page 59.

A.—UNIFORM (GENERAL).

(a) **Normal.**

Colour is *grey-green* (grigio-verde), although a medium grey drill is worn for fatigue duties. The style prescribed is the same for officers, W.Os., N.C.Os. and men, and is as follows:—

Head-dress (*Copricapo*).—Grey-green fatigue cap (*berretto a busta*)*
 or Steel helmet (*casco*).
Tunic (*Giubba*).—Grey-green, with open collar (no piping or embroidery, plain grey-green buttons).
Shirt (*Camicia*).—Grey-green, worn with collar and tie.
Knickerbockers (*Pantaloni corti*).—Grey-Green (no stripes).
†Puttees (*Fasce gambiere*).—Grey-green.
Boots (*Stivaletti*).—Black ammunition.

IMPORTANT NOTE

The adoption of the same style of uniform for all ranks (including officers) dates from special instructions issued in June, 1940. This permitted the retention and use of the former distinctive, more conspicuous and more costly styles, until stocks were exhausted or uniforms worn out. They may therefore still be encountered from time to time. Details are given in *Appendix* A.

---

* Except Alpini, Customs Guards, pack artillery personnel and Bersaglieri (*see* page 19).
† Cavalry, some artillery, tank and M.T. personnel wear black leggings (*gambali*).

(*b*) **Tropical.**

Khaki drill is worn. No information is available to show whether any special instructions were issued in June, 1940, but the style prescribed would seem to be the same for all ranks and to be as given below. It is evident, however, that considerable variation is practised and permitted.

Head-dress.—Khaki topee (Wolseley pattern).*
 or Steel helmet.

Tunic.—Khaki drill, with turn-down collar buttoning up to the neck.

†Leg-wear.—Khaki drill trousers fitting tightly above the ankles.

Boots.—Black ammunition.

B.—BADGES OF ARM AND REGIMENTAL NUMBERS

The *badge* (fregio) *of arm of service* is worn on the front of all types of *head-dress* (stencilled in the case of steel helmets); also probably on the shoulder-straps of officers *in tropical uniform*.

The *regimental number* should be found in the *centre of the boss* (*i.e.*, central circle) of this badge. The boss itself may be painted black for the Grenadiers, grey-green for the other fighting arms of the Metropolitan Army and bright green for colonial troops. For the Services the boss may be of the same colour as the characteristic device (*see* next paragraph); a cross is substituted for the number, and may also be worn by certain H.Q. personnel.

In addition, all *infantry regiments* of the line wear *coloured gorget patches* (called *mostrine*) on each side of the tunic collar, whilst *other arms and services* are distinguished by a variety of *coloured devices* (called generically *mostreggiature*).

The gorget patches and devices may be absent on tropical uniform; on the other hand, the badge of arm of service will probably be worn on the shoulder-straps of officers.

For details of these badges, patches and devices *see* pages 23-52.

IMPORTANT NOTE

Changes have occurred, in line with those applied to the uniform itself. Refer to *Appendix* B for details of the former additional distinguishing marks, which may still be encountered.

---

* Other types of head-dress may often be encountered.
† Breeches or knickerbockers are also worn, with puttees, leggings or stockings. Shorts are likewise in evidence.

C.—BADGES OF RANK (*Distintivi di grado*).

(*a*) *Officers*.—Normally worn on the cuff and on the head-dress, except the steel helmet (*see* pages 54-56). *In tropical uniform, on the shoulder-strap* (*controspallina*) (*see* pages 21 and 54-56). If in any circumstances shirt-sleeve uniform is being worn, the rank badge may appear above the left breast-pocket.

(*b*) *W.Os*.—Always on the shoulder-strap and on the head-dress, except the steel helmet (*see* pages 58-59).

(*c*) *N.C.Os*.—On the sleeve only (*see* pages 58-59).

IMPORTANT NOTE

Changes have occurred, in line with those applied to the uniform itself. Refer to *Appendix C* for details of rank badges previously worn; these may still be encountered.

D.—" PAY BOOK."

This is called a *libretto personale* and corresponds roughly, in the case of *N.C.Os. and men*, to our A.B. 64. It records age, name, rank, number and unit (down to company or equivalent level), and contains many other interesting particulars regarding the holder's civil and military history and accomplishments. It also gives details of the arms, equipment and clothing on issue to him. It does not, in point of fact, serve as a pay book. One *libretto* only is issued to cover the whole of a soldier-citizen's military career.

The book carried by *officers and W.Os*. is almost exclusively a pay book and is renewed each year. Much less information is obtainable from it, but age, name, rank and unit are recorded.

Specimen pages from both types of *libretto* are given in *Appendix* D.

E.—IDENTITY PLATE.

Called a *piastrina* (or *medaglioncino*) *di riconoscimento*. It is worn on a chain round the neck. It is made of cheap metal and records name, number, religion, year of conscript class (*i.e.*, age), home town and province, all stamped in relief.

With the aid of a pen-knife or similar instrument, it can be split lengthwise into two identical plates.

Variations in the order in which the particulars are recorded occur, but a typical specimen is shown in *Appendix E*.

13

UNIFORM AS WORN BY OFFICERS AND OTHER RANKS
SUBSEQUENT TO JUNE 1940.

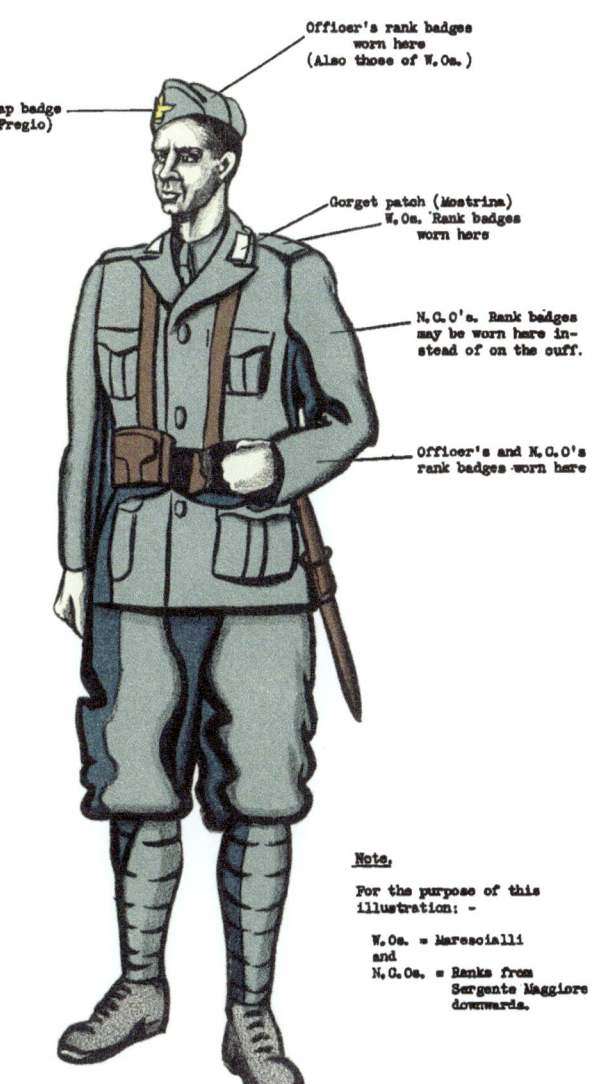

Officer's rank badges worn here
(Also those of W.Os.)

Cap badge (Fregio)

Gorget patch (Mostrina)
W.Os. Rank badges worn here

N.C.O's. Rank badges may be worn here instead of on the cuff.

Officer's and N.C.O's rank badges worn here

Note.

For the purpose of this illustration: -

W.Os. = Marescialli
and
N.C.Os. = Ranks from Sergente Maggiore downwards.

3537

ITALIAN OFFICERS

(Left: a Second-Lieutenant of Infantry, exhibiting shoulder-strap with badge of arm, *not now worn*; gorget patch with five-pointed star; rank badge above cuff; divisional escutcheon on left arm, *not now worn*.

Right: a Lieutenant of the Bersaglieri, with shoulder-strap, *not now worn*, and gorget device—two-pointed deep-crimson flame, with five-pointed star. His forage cap illustrates the system of showing rank on this type of head-dress.)

ITALIAN INFANTRY SOLDIERS

The one on the left is wearing the regulation fatigue cap, the one on the right the peace-time forage cap. Both have black collars and divisional escutcheons on left arm, neither of which are now worn.

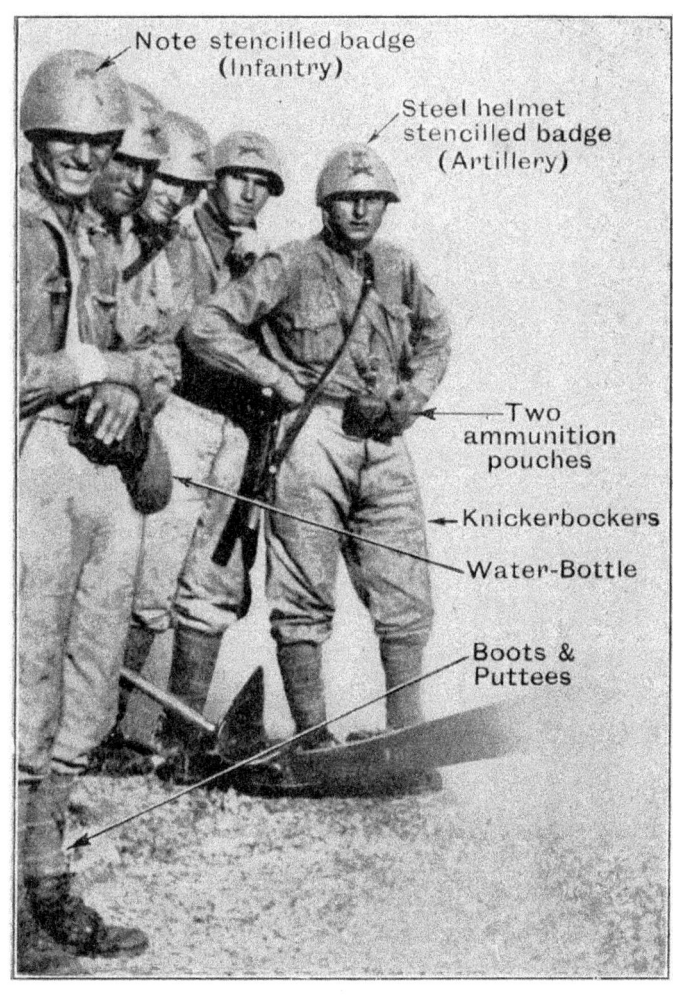

ITALIAN TROOPS in shirtsleeves

Distinctive Head-dresses

ALPINI

A similar hat may be worn by Customs Guards, all pack artillery personnel and Blackshirt militiamen.

BERSAGLIERI

(*Note.*—The plumes are also worn on steel helmets)

ALPINI SOLDIER

ITALIAN OFFICER IN TROPICAL UNIFORM

(Badges of arm—M.T. Corps—and rank—Captain—
on shoulder-strap; five-pointed star only on collar.
Note.—Shoulder-strap is black with blue piping; plain
khaki is more probable at the present time.)

VARIOUS STYLES IN TROPICAL WEAR

(Top left: shows fatigue cap with badge of arm—Commissariat—and forage cap with badge of arm—M.T. Corps. In each case the five-pointed star is on the collar.

Top right: shows topee with badge of arm—Infantry; also shoulder-strap with badges of arm and of rank—Lieutenant, *and* infantry gorget patch with five-pointed star. *Note.*—Shoulder-strap is black with red piping; plain khaki is more probable at the present time. Furthermore, the gorget patch may be absent.

Bottom: shows artillery personnel wearing topees).

GORGET PATCHES AND DEVICES

These are in colours and are worn on each side of the collar just above the lapel. They measure 60 x 32 mm. and take the following forms: —

(a) **Rectangles** (*Mostrine*). Plain or striped (*see* pages 25-29). When used alone, they denote divisional infantry. On the other hand, when they carry another device (*see* below) superimposed upon them, they indicate the divisional unit of the arm of the service characterized by that device.

(*Note.*—Plain green and plain blue rectangles, which characterize Alpini and mechanized troops respectively, are used in this connection *only* as a background for other devices, but it so happens that these colours denote Infantry Regiments 51-52 and 23-24 (*see* pages 25 and 27). Careful discrimination is necessary in these cases.

(b) **Braids** (*Alamari*). Worn on a coloured background by the Carabinieri Reali, the Sardegna Grenadiers and the General Staff (*see* page 37). The Grenadier patches have precisely the same significance as the infantry rectangles and may also be used in combination with another device.

(c) **Single-pointed flames** (*Fiamme ad una punta*). Denote artillery, engineers, various services, Frontier Guard, territorial and garrison troops, and are in plain colours or in black or green with coloured background or coloured piping (*see* pages 37-39). As explained above, they may be superimposed upon rectangles or braid.

(d) **Two-pointed flames** (*Fiamme a due punte*). Worn by Alpini, Bersaglieri, tank units, M.T. Corps and Customs Guards (*see* page 39).

(e) **Three-pointed flames** (*Fiamme a tre punte*).—Worn only by the cavalry (*see* page 33).

(f) **Chemical device.** For all chemical warfare and decontamination troops (*see* page 37). May be superimposed upon rectangles or braid to denote the unit belonging to a particular formation.

Study carefully the examples of combined patches and devices given on page 41.

Observe that a rectangular *background* of green always denotes Alpini and, similarly, that a rectangular *background* of blue always denotes mechanization, except as stated in the *Note* to sub-paragraph (a) above.

Bear in mind that all these identifications *may be absent on tropical uniform.*

GORGET PATCHES OF INFANTRY LINE REGIMENTS

NOTES

1. There has been no change in the designs of these patches. *Prior to June*, 1940, however, the size prescribed was slightly different and, moreover, the patch was worn on a *black collar*, round the outer edge of which officers had thin red piping. They had this same piping at the cuffs and also wore broad black stripes with red piping in the centre down each side of their breeches.

2. The five-pointed star (*see* Note 2, page 10) is worn in the centre of the rectangle close to the lower edge.

25

GORGET PATCHES OF INFANTRY LINE REGIMENTS.

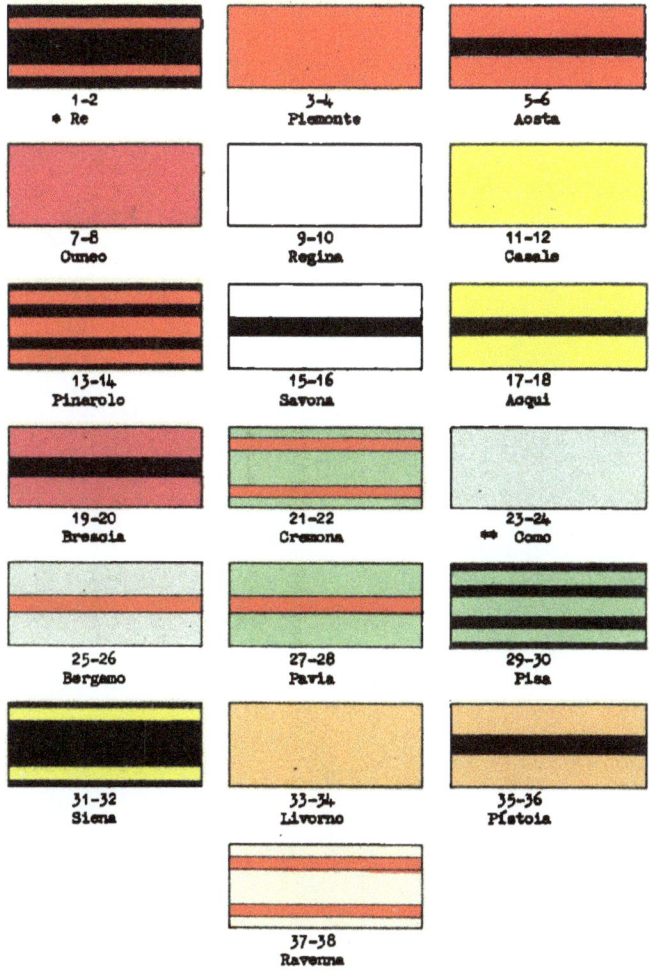

1-2 * Re
3-4 Piemonte
5-6 Aosta
7-8 Cuneo
9-10 Regina
11-12 Casale
13-14 Pinerolo
15-16 Savona
17-18 Acqui
19-20 Brescia
21-22 Cremona
23-24 ** Como
25-26 Bergamo
27-28 Pavia
29-30 Pisa
31-32 Siena
33-34 Livorno
35-36 Pistoia
37-38 Ravenna

* May wear a red tie
** May wear a blue tie

27

GORGET PATCHES OF INFANTRY. (Contd.)

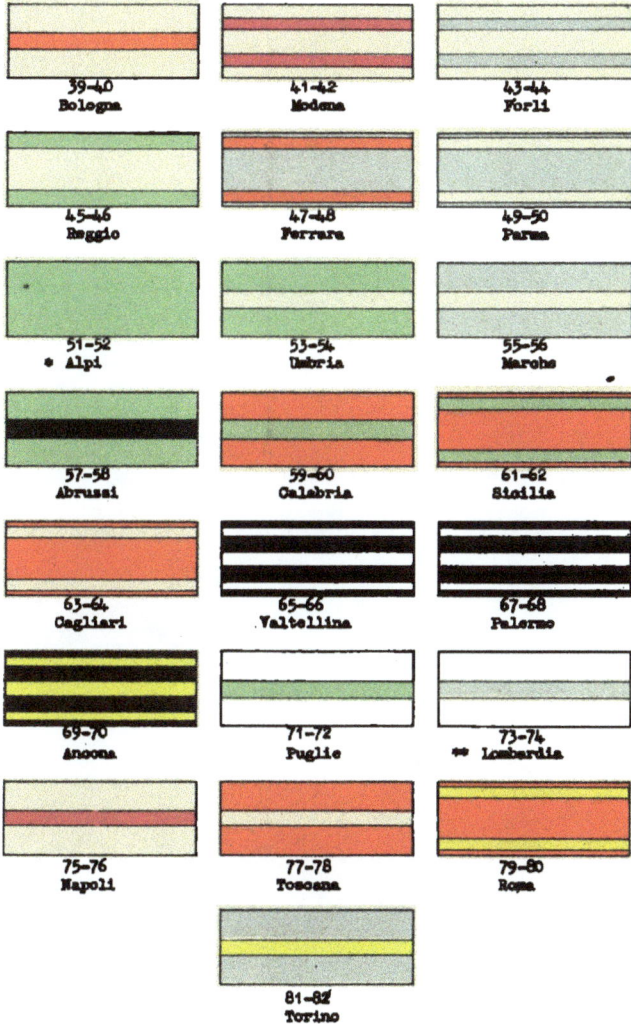

* May wear a red tie
** May wear a blue tie

GORGET PATCHES OF INFANTRY. (Contd.)

83-84 Venezia	85-86 Verona	87-88 Friuli
89-90 Salerno	91-92 Basilicata	93-94 Messina
95-96 Udine	97-98 Genova	115-116 Treviso
125-126 Spezia ?	127-128 Firenze ?	139-140 Bari ?
141-142 Catanzaro	151-152 Sassari	157-158 Liguria
207-208 ?	213-214 Arno	217-218 ?
225-226	231-232	Div. M.G Bns.

GORGET DEVICES OF CAVALRY REGIMENTS

NOTES

1. All devices shown are those prescribed *since June, 1940*.

2. *Prior to that date,* the following more conspicuous distinguishing marks were worn:—

   (a) In the case of numbers 1, 4, 5, 6 and 9, complete collars (plain, without device) in the respective colours.
   (b) For number 2, a complete scarlet collar with thin black edging.
   (c) For number 3, a complete black collar with thin scarlet edging.
   (d) In the case of numbers 10, 11, 12, 13 and 14, complete collars in the respective base colours, instead of rectangles only, with three-pointed flames in the colours as shown for the present flames.
   (e) For number 7, a complete crimson collar with thin black edging.
   (f) For number 8, a complete orange collar with thin black edging.
   (g) For number 15, a complete plain orange collar.

3. The five-pointed star (*see* Note 2, page 10) is worn on the patch, below the point where the flames separate.

33

GORGET DEVICES OF CAVALRY REGIMENTS

1.

1st - Nizza
(Crimson)

2.

2nd - Piemonte
(Scarlet on black)

3.

3rd - Savoia
(Black velvet)

4.

4th - Genova
(Deep yellow)

5.

5th - Novara
(White)

6.

6th - Aosta
(Scarlet)

7.

7th - Milano
(Crimson on black)

8.

9th - Firenze
(Orange on black)

9.

10th - Vitt. Em. II
(Yellow)

10.

12th - Saluzzo
(Black on yellow)

11.

13th - Monferrato
(Crimson on black)

12.

14th - Alessandria
(Orange on black)

13.

19th - Guide
(White on sky-blue)

14.

"Sardegna" Sqn.
(White on scarlet)

15.

Cavalry School
Horse training and
breeding depots
(Orange)

GORGET PATCHES AND DEVICES OF ARMS AND SERVICES

other than infantry of the line and cavalry

NOTES

1. *Prior to June,* 1940, the characteristic colours were the same as is now the case. Flames had one or two points, just as at present, but were rather more elaborate. Furthermore, all patches and devices were worn upon a complete black or coloured collar.

2. If still encountered, these more conspicuous distinguishing marks should be immediately recognizable.

3. The five-pointed star (*see* Note 2, page 10) is worn on the patch or device, in the same way as for the infantry of the line and the cavalry.

GORGET PATCHES AND DEVICES OF ARMS AND SERVICES

other than infantry of the line and cavalry

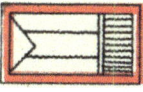

Carabinieri Reali
(Scarlet background)

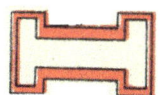

Granatieri di Sardegna
(White on scarlet background)

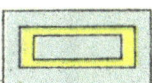

General Staff *
(Yellow on blue background)

Non-divisional infantry
(Fanteria fuori corpo)
or area troops
(distrettuali)
(Dark blue on scarlet background)

Chemical device
(Scarlet flame)

Artillery (and animal
transport personnel)
(Black on yellow-orange)

Engineers
(Black on
deep crimson)

Administration Service
(Black with blue piping)

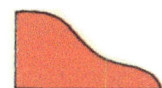

Territorial and garrison
troops
(Scarlet)

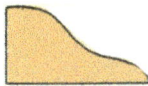

Mobile territorial
troops
(Yellow-orange)

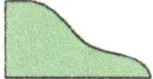

Alpini garrison
troops
(Green)

* Officers <u>attached</u> to the General Staff wear as a background to the yellow braid the infantry gorget patch (or Grenadier braid) or the flame of arm or service to which they belong.

GORGET PATCHES AND DEVICES OF ARMS AND SERVICES

other than infantry and cavalry (contd.)

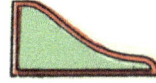

Frontier Guard infantry
(including M.G. personnel)
(Green on red)

Frontier Guard artillery
(Green on yellow-orange)

Frontier Guard Engineers
(Green on deep crimson)

Commissariat Service
(Violet)

Supply Service
(Deep sky-blue)

Medical Service
and Pharmacists
(Magenta)

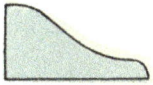

Veterinary Service
(Sky-blue)

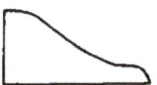

Fencing Masters
(White)

Alpini
(Green)

Bersaglieri
(Deep crimson)

Customs Guard
(Yellow)

Infantry tanks
(Scarlet on blue)

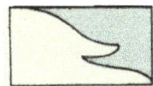

Light tanks of Mobile
Divisions
(White on blue)

M.T. Corps
(Black on blue)

3537.

EXAMPLES OF COMBINED GORGET PATCHES AND DEVICES

Artillery of 31st
(Calabria) Division
(Inf. Regts. 59 and 60)

Engineers of
31st Division

Medical unit of
31st Division

Supply unit of
31st Division

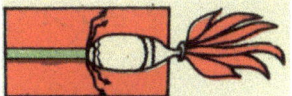

Chemical unit of
31st Division

Medical unit of
21st (Granatieri
di Sardegna) Division

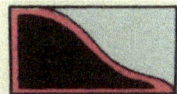

Engineers of motorised
or armoured divisions
(or of 14th - Isonzo -
Division)

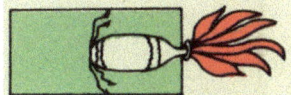

Chemical unit
of Alpini
* (or of 22nd -
Cacciatori delle
Alpi - Division)

Chemical unit of
motorised or
armoured divisions
* (or of 14th -
Isonzo - Division)

* See Note to sub-section (a) page 23.

Note also:-

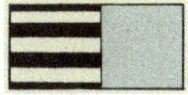

Infantry (65th and 66th Regts.)
of 101st (Trieste) Motorised
Division

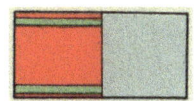

Infantry (61st and 62nd Regts.)
of 102nd (Trento) Motorised
Division

BADGES OF ARM OF SERVICE

NOTES

1. These are worn on all types of head-dress; on steel helmets they are stencilled.

2. Whereas, in peace time, officers' badges were embroidered (usually in gold upon a black background), the soldier's badge—in metal—is now prescribed for all ranks.

(*Exception*.—Badges Nos. 26-29, as worn by officers, are woven on black artificial silk.)

3. The *embroidered badges* may still be found on the shoulder-straps of *officers in tropical uniform*.

4. The number of the regiment may appear in the boss, or centre circle, of the badge, and the boss may be coloured as follows:—

Grenadiers	Black.
Other fighting arms of the Metropolitan Army.	Grey-green.
Colonial Troops	Bright green.
Services ...	Same colour as the gorget patch (*e.g.*, maroon for medical, violet for commissariat).

A cross is substituted for the number in the case of the services, or for certain H.Q. personnel.

Badges of Arm of Service

Infantry

1.

INFANTRY of the LINE

2.

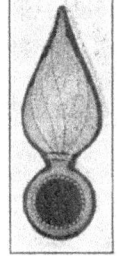

GRANATIERI
(*i.e.* Grenadiers)

3.

BERSAGLIERI

4.

ALPINI

5.

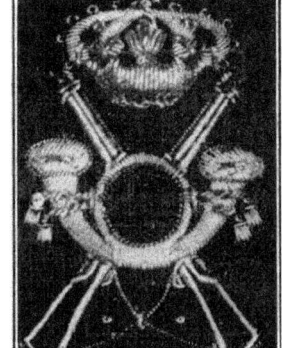

COLONIAL INFANTRY

Badges of Arm of Service—*continued*

Cavalry

6.

Nizza, Piemonte,
Savoia, Genova

7.

Novara, Aosta, Milano,
Firenze, Vittorio
Emanuele II

8.

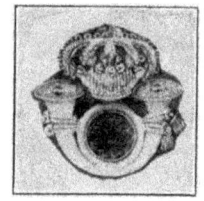

Saluzzo, Monferrato,
Alessandria, Guide,
Sardegna

Tanks

9.

TANK
INFANTRY
(*Fanteria carrista*)

10.

LIGHT TANKS
with
Mobile Divisions

Badges of Arm of Service—*continued*

Artillery

Note.—Crossed gun barrels, lying *flat*, are common to all artillery badges.

11.

ARMY ARTILLERY
(Note the 5 balls upon which the grenade of badge No. 11 rests. This distinguishes it from badge No. 12)

12.

CORPS ARTILLERY

13.

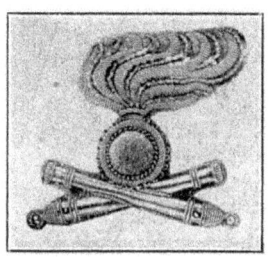

INFANTRY DIVISIONAL ARTILLERY

14.

ALPINI ARTILLERY
(Compare badge No. 4)

Badges of Arm of Service—*co: tinued*

15.

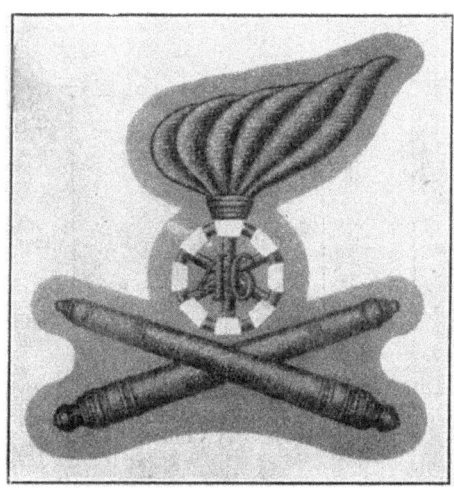

ARTILLERY
with Motorized Divisions

16.

A.A. ARTILLERY
(Note wings)

17.

ARTILLERY
with Mobile Divisions

18.

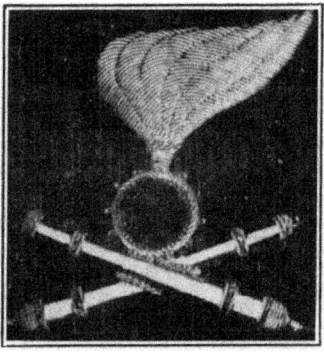

COLONIAL ARTILLERY

Badges of Arm of Service—*continued*

Engineers

Note.—Crossed axes are common to all Engineer badges.

19.

ENGINEERS
Field units

20.

ENGINEERS
Telegraph and Wireless units

21.

ENGINEERS
Bridging units

22.

ENGINEERS
Railway units

Badges of Arm of Service—*continued*

23.

Chemical Warfare Units

24.

COLONIAL ENGINEERS

Services

25.

26.

M.T. CORPS
(May have a *cross*, not a number, in the *centre circle*)

COMMISSARIAT

Badges of Arm of Service—*continued*

27.

ARTILLERY AND ENGINEER SERVICES: Silver cross on gold star.

MEDICAL: Red cross on silver star.

VETERINARY: Silver star—light blue centre.

ADMINISTRATION: Gold star—dark blue centre.

General Officers and Officers of the General Staff

28.

Note.—The General Staff badge of the *Blackshirt Militia* is somewhat similar, but the eagle is not quite the same and it is *not* surmounted by a crown.

Badges of Arm of Service—*continued*

29.

PHARMACISTS

Carabinieri

30.

Air Force

31.

Navy

32.

BADGES OF RANK

OFFICERS

Notes.

1. On active service and with *grey-green uniform,* officers' rank badges are worn: —

   (a) on the sleeve of the tunic or greatcoat, just above the cuff. They take the form of broad and/or narrow bands (called *galloni* and *galloncini* respectively) with a loop similar to that worn in the British Navy. All bands are 50 mm. long; broad bands have a width of 12 mm., narrow bands 5 mm.

   (b) on the fatigue cap (*berretto a busta*). Here the system is one of rectangles and stars.

2. These badges are illustrated on pages 55-56. Those worn by General Officers are in white artificial silk and include an ornamental design (called a *greca*) below the bands. Other officers have yellow artificial silk.

3. If, for any reason, a *forage cap* is worn as in peace time, the badge consists of continuous bands round the cap, just as for the sleeve but without the top loop.

4. *On the Alpini hat,* the system of bands is formed into one of chevrons worn on the left side point uppermost. *See* page 19 where a Lieut.-Colonel's badge is illustrated.

5. *In tropical uniform,* a system of stars with or without embroidery or braiding is adopted, likewise illustrated on pages 55-56. The badge is worn on the shoulder-strap, on which the badge of arm of service may also appear.

---

6. Rank badges of naval and air force officers are similar in every way to those of the army, except that the loop is replaced by a diamond in the case of the air force (cf. the Blackshirt Militia—page 65).

BADGES OF RANK - OFFICERS

Rank	Sleeve	Fatigue Cap	Shoulder-strap (Tropical uniform)	Equivalent British rank
Maresciallo d'Italia		4 stars		Field Marshal
Generale d'Armata		3 stars		General
Generale Designato d'Armata	(with crown)	2 stars		
Generale di Corpo d'Armata	(with crown)	2 stars		Lieutenant-General
Generale di Divisione or * Tenente Generale		2 stars		Major-General

3537

Rank	Sleeve	Fatigue cap	Shoulder-strap (Tropical uniform)	Equivalent British Rank
Generale di Brigata or *Maggiore-Generale		★		Brigadier
Colonnello		★ ★ ★	★★	Colonel
Tenente Colonnello		★ ★	★★	Lieutenant-Colonel
Maggiore		★	★	Major
Capitano		★ ★ ★	★★	Captain
Tenente		★ ★	★★	Lieutenant
Sottotenente		★	★	Second Lieutenant

* Rank exclusive to artillery, engineers and M.T. officers.

BADGES OF RANK

WARRANT OFFICERS AND N.C.Os.
Notes.

1. These badges are illustrated opposite. They are the same for grey-green and for tropical uniform.

2. W.Os. (*marescialli*) wear bands, 6 mm. wide, in yellow artificial silk—streaked in the centre with black—on the shoulder-strap of tunic and greatcoat, and on the fatigue cap.

3. Other ranks wear chevrons, whose wings are 25 mm. long, either point upwards just above the cuff, or point downwards above the elbow, on both tunic and greatcoat. The chevrons of *sergenti maggiori* and *sergenti* are in *yellow artificial silk;* the *remainder* in *red artificial silk.*

BADGES OF RANK - WARRANT OFFICERS AND N.C.Os.

Rank	Sleeve	Shoulder-strap **	Equivalent British Rank.
* Maresciallo Maggiore	—		W.O. Class I
* Maresciallo Capo	—		W.O. Class I
* Maresciallo	—		W.O. Class II
* Sergente Maggiore (or Brigadiere of Carabinieri Reali or Customs Guard)		—	Staff Serjeant
* Sergente (or Vice-Brigadiere of Carabinieri Reali or Sotto-Brigadiere of Customs Guard)		—	Serjeant
Caporalmaggiore (or Guardia scelta of Customs Guard)		—	Lance Serjeant (Corporal Major)
§ Caporale (or Appuntato of Carabinieri Reali or Guardia Comune of Customs Guard)		—	Corporal
Soldato scelto (or Carabiniere of Carabinieri Reali or Allievo of Customs Guard)		—	Lance Corporal

** In addition, all three ranks wear one yellow stripe, streaked in the centre with black, on the fatigue cap.

* Called "sottufficiali".

§ Called "graduati".

Miscellaneous Badges

Note.—Except where otherwise stated, all the badges listed below are worn on the *left arm*, above the elbow.

Divisional Badge (discontinued) (Scudetto divisionale)	*Despatch Rider* (Staffetta)
1.	2.

Black on scarlet cloth, with letter " S "

Machine Gunner (Mitragliere)	*Motor Cyclist M.G. Personnel* (Mitraglieri motociclisti)
3.	4.

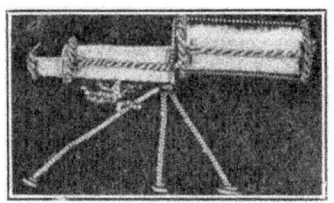 

Miscellaneous Badges —*continued*

Marksman (*not* necessarily
Bersagliere)
(Tiratore)

5.

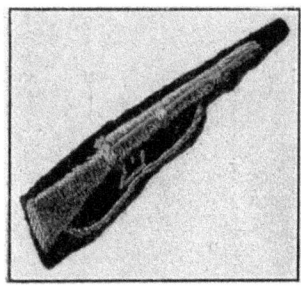

Mortar Personnel
(Mortieri)

6.

Miscellaneous Badges—*continued*

Army Personnel for Visual Communication to Aircraft

7.

Army Personnel for Wireless Communication to Aircraft

8.

Promotion for war merit
(Promozione per merito di guerra)

9.

(Worn on the *left breast*)

Air Observer (Army Personnel)
(Osservatore aereo)

10.

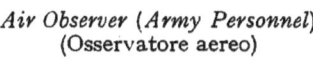

(Worn on the *left breast*)

Wound stripe

11.

Single gold (or yellow rayon) stripe, 1¾ in. long, worn at an angle on the *right arm* above the elbow.

Cockade

12.

A red, white and green cockade is sometimes worn on the *topee* as a back-ground to the badge of arm.

PART III

IDENTIFICATION OF BLACKSHIRT MILITIA PERSONNEL

Uniform.

Orders were issued to the Militia in June, 1940, as to the Army, whereby all ranks must wear the same style of uniform. This is substantially that of the army, thus normally grey-green, but is characterised by the wearing of black shirts and black ties. Khaki drill may be worn in hot climates. The fatigue cap is prescribed, although other types of head-dress may be found, notably a fez or a hat similar to that of the Alpini.

Branch of Service.

The Ordinary (*i.e.*, combatant) Militia trains only as infantry. No badge or arm of service, in the accepted sense of that term, is therefore worn. It is believed that all personnel of this Militia have a cap badge in black cloth as illustrated in Fig. 1 below. The name of a Blackshirt battalion may appear in the space in the centre; territorial cohorts will have a small black cross on a grey-green background in this space.

Blackshirts wear a two-pointed black flame as a gorget device. The personnel of territorial cohorts wear this flame on a scarlet rectangle (yellow-orange rectangle for *mobile* territorial cohorts). Note also that O.Rs. of territorial units, from Primo Caposquadra downwards, wear their unit number in Roman figures (white on black) on the shoulder-strap.

In all cases the Fascist symbol (Fig. 2) takes the place on the collar of the five-pointed star worn by the army. This is in gilded metal for General Officers and white metal for all other ranks.

FIG. 1.

FIG. 2.

Branches of the force other than the Ordinary (*i.e.*, combatant) Militia are distinguished, as far as is known, by colours on their facings as follows:—

Anti-aircraft and Coast Defence	Yellow.
Frontier	Green.
Forests	Green.
Railway	Crimson.
Roads	Bright blue.
Ports	Crimson.
Post and Telegraph	Crimson.
Medical Service	Maroon.
Administration Service	Blue.

Badges of rank.

These may be taken as identical, for all practical purposes, with those worn by equivalent ranks in the Army, in accordance with the table given below. Note, however, that:—

(a) General Officers wear red edging to their shoulder-straps and the *greca* is of a different design to that of General Officers in the Army, being as under:—

(b) the loop formed on the sleeve of army officers is substituted by a *diamond* in the case of the Militia.

Militia rank	Army rank
Luogotenente Generale ...	Generale di Divisione.
Console Generale	Generale di Brigata.
Console	Colonnello.
Primo Seniore	Tenente Colonnello.
Seniore	Maggiore.
Centurione...	Capitano.
Capomanipolo	Tenente.
Sottocapomanipolo ...	Sottotenente.
Primo Aiutante	Maresciallo Maggiore.
Secondo Aiutante ...	Maresciallo Capo.
Terzo Aiutante	Maresciallo.
†Primo Caposquadra ...	Sergente Maggiore.
†Caposquadra	Sergente.
Vicecaposquadra	Caporale Maggiore.
Camicia nera scelta ...	Caporale.

† Replaced by *Brigadiere* and *Vice Brigadiere* in certain branches of the force.

APPENDIX A

STYLE OF UNIFORM PRESCRIBED PRIOR TO JUNE, 1940

(a) Officers and W.Os.

Head-dress	*Grey-green forage cap (similar to the British Army pattern) with black patent leather peak.
Tunic	Grey-green, with black or coloured collars according to the arm of service, coloured piping also according to the arm of service (*see* pages 68-69) and metal buttons.
Shirt	Grey-green, with collar and tie.
Breeches	Grey-green, with stripes down each side and coloured piping according to the arm of service (*see* pages 68-69).
Boots	Black top *or* black ammunition, with grey-green puttees or stockings.†

(b) N.C.Os. and Men.

Head-dress	As under (*a*) above.
Tunic	Grey-green, with black or coloured collars, according to the arm of service.
Shirt	Grey-green, with collar and tie *or* zip-fastener.
Knickerbockers	Grey-green.
†Puttees	Grey-green.
Boots	Black ammunition.

---

* Except Alpini, Custom Guards, all pack artillery personnel and Bersaglieri (*see* page 19).

† Cavalry, some artillery, tank and M.T. personnel wore leggings.

APPENDIX B

BADGES OF ARM, FORMATION AND UNIT PRIOR TO JUNE, 1940

The badge of arm of service appeared on:—
  (i) the front of all types of head-dress (*maintained*);
  (ii) the shoulder-straps of officers, embroidered in **gold** thread (*discontinued*, except with tropical uniform).
  (iii) buttons, embossed (*discontinued*).

In addition, black or coloured collars (*discontinued*) denoted the arm of service, as well as the coloured gorget patch (*maintained*) or device (*modified*) worn on each side of the collar. Coloured piping at the cuffs and coloured stripes down the breeches of *officers* (*both discontinued*) still further distinguished the arm of service.

The *infantry* gorget patches were the same as they now are. This arm wore black collars, and red was the characteristic colour for piping and stripes.

As regards the *cavalry* collars and patches, refer to page 32.

For other arms *see* opposite.

Regimental numbers were worn in the centre of the boss on head-dress badges (*maintained*). Company numbers were worn by O.Rs. on the shoulder-strap (*discontinued*). Divisional escutcheons were worn on the left arm (*discontinued*).

COLLARS AND GORGET DEVICES OF ARMS
AND SERVICES
other than infantry of the line and cavalry

(Prior to June 1940).

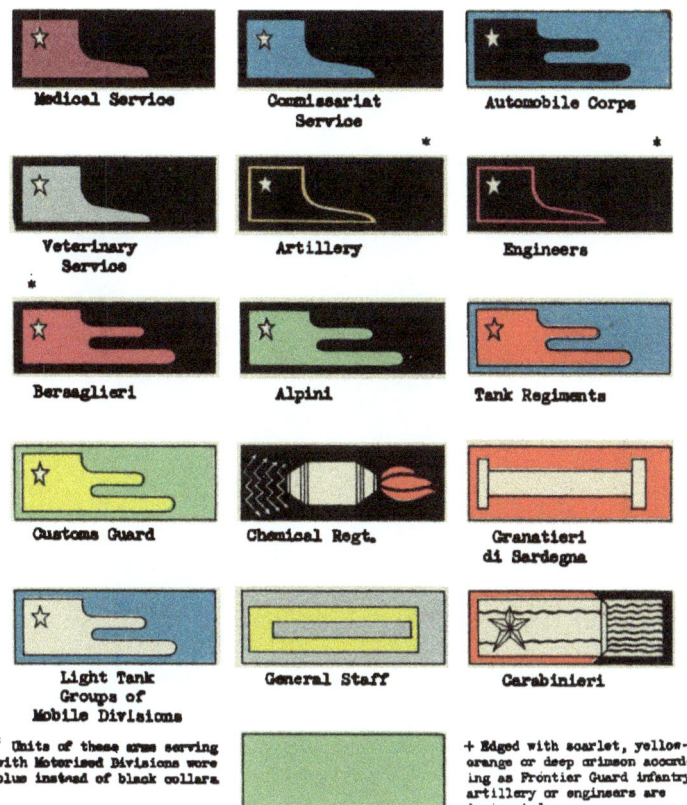

Medical Service

Commissariat Service

Automobile Corps

Veterinary Service

Artillery

Engineers

Bersaglieri

Alpini

Tank Regiments

Customs Guard

Chemical Regt.

Granatieri di Sardegna

Light Tank Groups of Mobile Divisions

General Staff

Carabinieri

Frontier Guard +

* Units of these arms serving with Motorised Divisions wore blue instead of black collars.

+ Edged with scarlet, yellow-orange or deep crimson according as Frontier Guard infantry, artillery or engineers are designated.

APPENDIX C

BADGES OF RANK PRIOR TO JUNE, 1940

Substantially the same as now, except that:—

(a) All badges were of larger size than prescribed in June, 1940.
(b) Silver and gold braid was used in place of white and yellow rayon (officers, W.Os. and N.C.Os. down to serjeants).
(c) Black braid was used instead of red rayon (N.C.Os. below the rank of serjeant).

APPENDIX D

PAY BOOKS

There are reproduced on the next eight pages: —

  (a) The front cover, pages 1-4 and page 6 of a *soldier's* " libretto personale "
  (b) The front cover and page 1 of an *officer's* " libretto personale "

in that order.

It will be seen that the front cover of the *soldier's book* shows his name, number, regiment and battery (the last two by rubber stamp). Many personal particulars are recorded on pages 1 and 2; page 3 deals with various phases of call up, promotion and release; page 4 again shows the battery and records transfer to another battery; page 5 refers to vaccination and inoculation. The book is a most valuable document to find on a prisoner.

The front cover of the *officer's book* gives no information. Page 1 shows the unit and sundry personal particulars. The book is not, however, of much practical value to an enemy.

N. 340 del Catal.
(R. 1938 - Anno XVI)

R. ESERCITO ITALIANO

(1) **10.° REGG.° ARTIGLIERIA C. d'A.**

10 Reggimento Art.ria C. d A
Truppe alla sede
1ª Batteria da 105/28

Libretto personale

di *Calabretta Domenicantru*

figlio di *Gregorio*

Distretto di ~~Catanzaro~~ *Roma*) classe 1920

Numero di matricola 4228

Ho prestato giuramento di fedeltà
ed onore il 21-4 anno XVIII

Il Comandante la Batteria

(1) Corpo, stabilimento o istituto militare.
(2) Compagnia, squadrone o batteria.

LIBRETTO PERSONALE

di *Calabretta Domenicantonio*
figlio di *Gregorio* e *fu Bruno Mariantonia*
nato addì *20-2* 19*20* nel Comune
di *S. Sostene* Provincia di *Catanzaro*
di religione *cattolica*
residente all'atto dell'arruolamento a *Roma*
Via *Giordani* N. *620*
Ufficio postale *Roma (30 Pignattera)*
inscritto nel Comune di *Roma*
Provincia di *Roma* Distretto militare
di ~~Catanzaro~~ *Roma ( ) Classe 19*20*
Ammogliato con ―――

il

Rimasto vedovo ―――
Professione o mestiere *Meccanico*
Grado d'istruzione e titolo di studio *5ª elementare*

(1) Cattolica, israelita, protestante ecc.
(2) Con autorizzazione del Comandante del ... appena prima di giungere all'arma.

A. — Contrassegni personali.

Statura m. 1, 80 Fronte *bassa*
Torace 0 92 Naso *grande*
Capelli { colore *biondi* Orecchie *piccole*
         { forma *lisci* Bocca *regolare*
Viso *ovale* Dentatura *guasta*
Colorito *roseo* Mento *piccolo*
Occhi *cerulei* Segni particolari
Sopracciglia *forti*

Difetti fisici che non esimono dal servizio

THIS PAGE IS NOT EXTRACTED FROM THE
"LIBRETTO PERSONALE" OF DOMENICANTONIO
CALABRETTA, BUT FROM THAT OF ANOTHER
SOLDIER WHOSE BOOK DISPLAYED MORE DE-
TAILED PARTICULARS

Gruppo sanguigno.

Residenza eletta all'invio in congedo e successive variazioni.

— 3 —

A. — Arruolamento, servizi, promozioni ed altre variazioni matricolari.

VARIAZIONI	DATA
Soldato di leva classe 1915 distretto Ferrara quale rivedibile e lasciato in congedo illimitato Deve rispondere alla chiamata alle armi della classe 1916	8 Maggio 1915
Chiamato alle armi e giunto al Distretto Militare di Bologna	17 Maggio 1935
Fate nel 10° Regg. Artigl. Pedonale	18 Maggio
Antigipre scelto in detto il	30 nov.
Fut. in detta il	3c Giugno 1935
Inviato in congedo illimitato per fine ferma	10 Novembre 1935

THIS PAGE IS NOT EXTRACTED FROM THE "LIBRETTO PERSONALE" OF DOMENICANTONIO CALABRETTA, BUT FROM THAT OF ANOTHER SOLDIER WHOSE BOOK DISPLAYED MORE DETAILED PARTICULARS

A. — Specializzazione.

Specializzazione

Corsi di abilitazione compiuti e risultato ottenuto

Qualifica ottenuta nella specializzazione

Assegnazioni e cambiamenti di reparto.

REPARTO	DATA
10 Reggimento Art.° C. d. A. Truppe alla sede 1ª Batteria da 105/28	11-3-940
265ª BATTERIA da 65.17 Artiglieria G. a F.	13 10 940

(1) In questo quadro va indicata la carica in cui si è specializzato il militare e in cui ha dimostrato maggiore attitudine durante il servizio militare, carica e attitudine che possono essere utili ai fini di eventuali richiami per esercitazioni e mobilitazione.

B. — Note sanitarie individuali.

Vaccinazione antivaiolosa - Stato antecedente

Vaccinazione e rivaccinazione	DATA			Esito	Firma dell'ufficiale medico
	Giorno	Mese	Anno		
1ª vaccinazione	8	4	1906		Dr. Ferro
2ª id.					
3ª id.					

Vaccinazione e rivaccinazione antitifica

Vaccino adoperato	DATA			Annotazioni	Firma dell'ufficiale medico
	Giorno	Mese	Anno		
1ª T.A.B.	1	4	40		
2ª " "	22	4	40		
3ª " "	7	5	40		

N. 2786 del Catal.
(1940 - Anno XVIII)

LIBRETTO PERSONALE

DEGLI

ASSEGNI E DELLE RITENUTE PER UFFICIALI MILITARIZZATI E MARESCIALLI

Ord. 1087 dell'11-6-1940-XVIII 300.000 - Ist. Ed. S. Michele - Roma

N. 2789 del Cat.
(1940 - Anno XVIII)

(1) 100° OSPEDALE DA CAMPO

LIBRETTO PERSONALE
DEGLI
ASSEGNI E DELLE RITENUTE
DI

Cognome e nome *Pirrone D. Francesco*
paternità di *Michele* nato a *Firenze*
il *9 Febbraio 1903* distretto militare
di *Pisa* Provincia di *Pisa*
grado militare *Tenente Farmacista* categoria *...*
impiego civile (2) *Aiuto Uffciciario R° Univers.tà P.sa*
amministrazione di provenienza (3) *R.a Università Pisa*
Stato di famiglia *coniugato con 3 figli*
Data d'impianto del libretto: *1° Agosto 1940 XVIII°*

FIRMA DEL TITOLARE

Visto per l'autenticità della firma
IL COMANDANTE DEL CORPO

(1) Corpo
(2) Solo per gl'impiegati e salariati degli enti indicati nell'art. 27 della legge sul trattamento economico di guerra
(3) Quella che ha pagato gli assegni civili sino al richiamo

APPENDIX E

Below is reproduced a typical identity plate:

Key—

1918	Year of birth, *i.e.*, conscript class.
2193	Number.
(19) ...	Code number of military district.
C	Catholic.
FRONTERA	Surname.
FRANCESCO	Christian name.
SALVATORE	Father's christian name.
MANCUSO	Mother's maiden name.
SAVERIA ...	Mother's christian name.
SAVELLI ...	Home town.
(CATANZARO)...	Province.

(B41/335) 20000 11/41 W.O.P. 8425

APPENDIX F

ITALIAN ORDERS AND DECORATIONS

Order or decoration	Ribbon (Actual normal size, reduced to 12 x 5 mm, on active service.)	Approximate British equivalent.
Ordine Militare di Savoia (High officers only).		G.C.V.O.
San Maurizio e San Lazzaro.		C.B.
Cavaliere Corona d'Italia.		O.B.E.
Valor Militare:- (with gold star) (with silver star) (with bronze star)		V.C. D.S.O. or D.C.M. M.C. or M.M.
Croce di Guerra (One given for each year's service; with palm for mention in despatches)		-
Libia 1911 - 1912		-

Note:- If the same decoration is awarded a second or third time, additional ribbons are worn; e.g., where a British officer with the M.C. and two bars would wear one ribbon and two rosettes, the Italian officer would wear three Valor Militare medals, each with its bronze star.

APPENDIX F

ITALIAN ORDERS AND DECORATIONS

Order or decoration	Ribbon (Actual normal size, reduced to 12 x 5 mm. on active service.)	Approximate British equivalent.
Guerra Mondiale 1915-1918 (with one silver star for each year's service).		-
Abissinia 1935-1936 (with palm for actual fighting).		-
Spagna 1938-1939.		-
Unita d'Italia		-
Marcia su Roma.		-
Long service (16 years; with crown in centre after 25 years).		-

Note:- If the same decoration is awarded a second or third time, additional ribbons are worn; e.g., where a British officer with the M.C. and two bars would wear one ribbon and two rosettes, the Italian officer would wear three Valor Militare medals, each with its bronze star.

www.ingramcontent.com/pod-product-compliance
Lightning Source LLC
Chambersburg PA
CBHW040302170426
43193CB00021B/2979